One Season
at a Time

Journal for Self-discovery

Blue hyacinth edition

One Season at a Time; Journal for Self-discovery

Blue hyacinth edition

Identifier: ISBN: 978-1-7364560-4-0 (softcover) First edition published 2022

Cover design by E. B. Lee

Photographs by E. B. Lee; watercolor renderings created by E. B. Lee with Waterlogue

Publishing Services: Little Brown Dog Press, Pinehurst, NC, USA, www. littlebrowndogpress.com

ONE SEASON AT A TIME

YOUR UNIQUE JOURNAL

For reflections, affirmations, goals, do-overs, gratitude, planning, and other daily wishes.

Let yourself grow

As an author, I know the power of words and the benefit of taking note of little things in life. Details.

I also recognize the incredible value derived from mindfully exploring events, feelings, and actions from any given day. Journals and jot journals are remarkable and easy places to make this happen. They are like super life organizers that nurture you heart, mind, and soul.

By taking a few minutes to collect thoughts of our daily lives – actually set them to paper in front of us - we immediately open ourselves to gaining greater control and understanding. We identify what is floating around (or racing around) our mind or heart, and make it visually manageable. It rests on paper, waiting for us to grasp, and calls on us to explore, consider, and become enlightened by it. It lets us organize it, set goals for it and around it, dismiss it if we wish, make plans for it, revel in a sense of accomplishment or gratitude for whatever it might be. We can create a framework to move forward with it or without it in a more compartmentalized form, rather than a floating thought. It helps us discover more about ourselves and appreciate our place in this daily puzzle, heightening our sense of self-worth, courage and acceptance, no matter what life throws our way. Even a careful look at our "want-to-do-overs" is valuable time spent.

I have journaled on and off throughout life. At times, I kept a formal journal – an actual book. At other times, I simply put pen to sheets of paper. Often, I created travel journals as recordings of new worlds I saw and experienced. Now, I jot. Less elaborate, but powerful.

Here's an interesting fact: I don't save my journals for long. Not as actual physical pages, that is. But I do believe I incorporate their best lessons within myself and carry these inside me as a part of the human I reinvent daily.

So... Pause... Please...

LET ONE SEASON AT A TIME

Help you find beauty and gratitude

This journal overflows with flowers. As a former flower farmer, I know flowers positively impact people. Studies back this up. Within these pages I share flowers I have grown and come upon otherwise.

What better way to create a positive mindset and establish powerful personal affirmations, gratitude and attributes – enabling ongoing growth - than surrounded by natural beauty?

Please, let these flowers lead you to thoughtful self-reflection, vibrancy, love, and appreciation, along with a determination to make each day better than the last, to build a meaningful future one day at a time.

Every flower begins as a bud.

~

Help you pause

There is something special about the fuzzy outlines and soft appearance of watercolor renderings, which make you look at them differently than you look at a photograph with realistic lines, colors and clarity. They make you pause, even if only for a moment.

I created these watercolors with photographs and computer program. This astounds me. I am a pen to paper sort of person, but I find the results pleasing. I hope you do too.

So, go ahead. Pause. Let this special presentation seep in and unlatch a part of you that lies within, beyond your usual boundaries.

Waves roll in and waves roll out, pausing in between transitions.

Help you see the world with different eyes

Let the power of a jot journal and a few minutes of time move you to see and feel gratitude and live with a sense of increased clarity.

Reach within to see differently around you.
Reach beyond to find brand new opportunities within.

~

Organize and grow

Every few months, I look back through the pages of the season. I see just how much I have faced, considered, accomplished, and grown, even as I felt I was treading along day by day, often task by task. This seasonal look makes me appreciate just how rich life is and how worthy I am, even at times when I have struggled, because I have moved forward in the best ways I could. Writing this down lets me separate some of the emotional cover, which can obscure facts and the possibilities to live a full life.

Whether you use this as a daily planner, gratitude journal, or place for inner thoughts,
please, grant yourself a few minutes a day
– or a few minutes every few days –
to express yourself for YOU and you alone.
Grab a pen or pencil and begin.

Whether you prefer to start your days with a few thoughts on paper, use night time as your quiet time, or like to use both ends of a day to gather your thoughts, enjoy your journey!

Welcome!

Day of the week _____ Date _____

GOALS - PLANS - FEELINGS - THOUGHTS - SELF-AFFIRMATIONS
DO-OVER WISHES
ALL GO HERE
FOR YOU!

THANKING MY LUCKY STARS FOR:

_____

_____

_____

LOVE THAT I DID THIS TODAY OR HAVE THIS PLANNED FOR THE DAY:

_____

_____

MAYBE THIS COULD BE IMPROVED:

_____

_____

YES, I ROCK! HERE'S AN AFFIRMATION TO BACK THIS UP:

_____

GOALS ARE GOOD:

_____

_____

JUST HAD TO ADD THIS:

_____

_____

Welcome Back!

Day of the week _____ Date _____

GOALS - PLANS - FEELINGS - THOUGHTS - SELF-AFFIRMATIONS
DO-OVER WISHES
ALL GO HERE
FOR YOU!

THANKING MY LUCKY STARS FOR:

_____

_____

_____

LOVE THAT I DID THIS TODAY OR HAVE THIS PLANNED FOR THE DAY:

_____

_____

MAYBE THIS COULD BE IMPROVED:

_____

_____

YES, I ROCK! HERE'S AN AFFIRMATION TO BACK THIS UP:

_____

GOALS ARE GOOD:

_____

_____

JUST HAD TO ADD THIS:

_____

_____

Welcome Back!

Day of the week _____ Date _____

GOALS - PLANS - FEELINGS - THOUGHTS - SELF-AFFIRMATIONS
DO-OVER WISHES
ALL GO HERE
FOR YOU!

THANKING MY LUCKY STARS FOR:

_____

_____

_____

LOVE THAT I DID THIS TODAY OR HAVE THIS PLANNED FOR THE DAY:

_____

_____

MAYBE THIS COULD BE IMPROVED:

_____

_____

YES, I ROCK! HERE'S AN AFFIRMATION TO BACK THIS UP:

_____

GOALS ARE GOOD:

_____

_____

JUST HAD TO ADD THIS:

_____

_____

Welcome Back!

Day of the week _____ Date _____

GOALS - PLANS - FEELINGS - THOUGHTS - SELF-AFFIRMATIONS
DO-OVER WISHES
ALL GO HERE
FOR YOU!

THANKING MY LUCKY STARS FOR:

_____

_____

_____

LOVE THAT I DID THIS TODAY OR HAVE THIS PLANNED FOR THE DAY:

_____

_____

MAYBE THIS COULD BE IMPROVED:

_____

_____

YES, I ROCK! HERE'S AN AFFIRMATION TO BACK THIS UP:

_____

GOALS ARE GOOD:

_____

_____

JUST HAD TO ADD THIS:

_____

_____

4

Welcome Back!

Day of the week _____ Date _____

GOALS - PLANS - FEELINGS - THOUGHTS - SELF-AFFIRMATIONS
DO-OVER WISHES
ALL GO HERE
FOR YOU!

THANKING MY LUCKY STARS FOR:

_____

_____

_____

LOVE THAT I DID THIS TODAY OR HAVE THIS PLANNED FOR THE DAY:

_____

_____

MAYBE THIS COULD BE IMPROVED:

_____

_____

YES, I ROCK! HERE'S AN AFFIRMATION TO BACK THIS UP:

_____

GOALS ARE GOOD:

_____

_____

JUST HAD TO ADD THIS:

_____

_____

Welcome Back!

Day of the week _____ Date _____

GOALS - PLANS - FEELINGS - THOUGHTS - SELF-AFFIRMATIONS
DO-OVER WISHES
ALL GO HERE
FOR YOU!

THANKING MY LUCKY STARS FOR:

_____

_____

_____

LOVE THAT I DID THIS TODAY OR HAVE THIS PLANNED FOR THE DAY:

_____

_____

MAYBE THIS COULD BE IMPROVED:

_____

_____

YES, I ROCK! HERE'S AN AFFIRMATION TO BACK THIS UP:

_____

GOALS ARE GOOD:

_____

_____

JUST HAD TO ADD THIS:

_____

_____

Welcome Back!

Day of the week _____ Date _____

GOALS - PLANS - FEELINGS - THOUGHTS - SELF-AFFIRMATIONS
DO-OVER WISHES
ALL GO HERE
FOR YOU!

THANKING MY LUCKY STARS FOR:

_____

_____

_____

LOVE THAT I DID THIS TODAY OR HAVE THIS PLANNED FOR THE DAY:

_____

_____

MAYBE THIS COULD BE IMPROVED:

_____

_____

YES, I ROCK! HERE'S AN AFFIRMATION TO BACK THIS UP:

_____

GOALS ARE GOOD:

_____

_____

JUST HAD TO ADD THIS:

_____

_____

Welcome Back!

Day of the week _____ Date _____

GOALS - PLANS - FEELINGS - THOUGHTS - SELF-AFFIRMATIONS
DO-OVER WISHES
ALL GO HERE
FOR YOU!

THANKING MY LUCKY STARS FOR:

_____

_____

_____

LOVE THAT I DID THIS TODAY OR HAVE THIS PLANNED FOR THE DAY:

_____

_____

MAYBE THIS COULD BE IMPROVED:

_____

_____

YES, I ROCK! HERE'S AN AFFIRMATION TO BACK THIS UP:

_____

GOALS ARE GOOD:

_____

_____

JUST HAD TO ADD THIS:

_____

_____

Welcome Back!

Day of the week _____ Date _____

GOALS - PLANS - FEELINGS - THOUGHTS - SELF-AFFIRMATIONS
DO-OVER WISHES
ALL GO HERE
FOR YOU!

THANKING MY LUCKY STARS FOR:

_____

_____

_____

LOVE THAT I DID THIS TODAY OR HAVE THIS PLANNED FOR THE DAY:

_____

_____

MAYBE THIS COULD BE IMPROVED:

_____

_____

YES, I ROCK! HERE'S AN AFFIRMATION TO BACK THIS UP:

_____

GOALS ARE GOOD:

_____

_____

JUST HAD TO ADD THIS:

_____

_____

Welcome Back!

Day of the week _____ Date _____

GOALS - PLANS - FEELINGS - THOUGHTS - SELF-AFFIRMATIONS
DO-OVER WISHES
ALL GO HERE
FOR YOU!

THANKING MY LUCKY STARS FOR:

_____

_____

_____

LOVE THAT I DID THIS TODAY OR HAVE THIS PLANNED FOR THE DAY:

_____

_____

MAYBE THIS COULD BE IMPROVED:

_____

_____

YES, I ROCK! HERE'S AN AFFIRMATION TO BACK THIS UP:

_____

GOALS ARE GOOD:

_____

_____

JUST HAD TO ADD THIS:

_____

_____

Welcome Back!

Day of the week _____ Date _____

GOALS - PLANS - FEELINGS - THOUGHTS - SELF-AFFIRMATIONS
DO-OVER WISHES
ALL GO HERE
FOR YOU!

THANKING MY LUCKY STARS FOR:

_____

_____

_____

LOVE THAT I DID THIS TODAY OR HAVE THIS PLANNED FOR THE DAY:

_____

_____

MAYBE THIS COULD BE IMPROVED:

_____

_____

YES, I ROCK! HERE'S AN AFFIRMATION TO BACK THIS UP:

_____

GOALS ARE GOOD:

_____

_____

JUST HAD TO ADD THIS:

_____

_____

Welcome Back!

Day of the week _____ Date _____

GOALS - PLANS - FEELINGS - THOUGHTS - SELF-AFFIRMATIONS
DO-OVER WISHES
ALL GO HERE
FOR YOU!

THANKING MY LUCKY STARS FOR:

_____

_____

_____

LOVE THAT I DID THIS TODAY OR HAVE THIS PLANNED FOR THE DAY:

_____

_____

MAYBE THIS COULD BE IMPROVED:

_____

_____

YES, I ROCK! HERE'S AN AFFIRMATION TO BACK THIS UP:

_____

GOALS ARE GOOD:

_____

_____

JUST HAD TO ADD THIS:

_____

_____

14

Welcome Back!

Day of the week _____ Date _____

GOALS - PLANS - FEELINGS - THOUGHTS - SELF-AFFIRMATIONS
DO-OVER WISHES
ALL GO HERE
FOR YOU!

THANKING MY LUCKY STARS FOR:

_____

_____

_____

LOVE THAT I DID THIS TODAY OR HAVE THIS PLANNED FOR THE DAY:

_____

_____

MAYBE THIS COULD BE IMPROVED:

_____

_____

YES, I ROCK! HERE'S AN AFFIRMATION TO BACK THIS UP:

_____

GOALS ARE GOOD:

_____

_____

JUST HAD TO ADD THIS:

_____

_____

Welcome Back!

Day of the week _____ Date _____

GOALS - PLANS - FEELINGS - THOUGHTS - SELF-AFFIRMATIONS
DO-OVER WISHES
ALL GO HERE
FOR YOU!

THANKING MY LUCKY STARS FOR:

_____

_____

_____

LOVE THAT I DID THIS TODAY OR HAVE THIS PLANNED FOR THE DAY:

_____

_____

MAYBE THIS COULD BE IMPROVED:

_____

_____

YES, I ROCK! HERE'S AN AFFIRMATION TO BACK THIS UP:

_____

GOALS ARE GOOD:

_____

_____

JUST HAD TO ADD THIS:

_____

_____

Welcome Back!

Day of the week _____ Date _____

GOALS - PLANS - FEELINGS - THOUGHTS - SELF-AFFIRMATIONS
DO-OVER WISHES
ALL GO HERE
FOR YOU!

THANKING MY LUCKY STARS FOR:

_____

_____

_____

LOVE THAT I DID THIS TODAY OR HAVE THIS PLANNED FOR THE DAY:

_____

_____

MAYBE THIS COULD BE IMPROVED:

_____

_____

YES, I ROCK! HERE'S AN AFFIRMATION TO BACK THIS UP:

_____

GOALS ARE GOOD:

_____

_____

JUST HAD TO ADD THIS:

_____

_____

Welcome Back!

Day of the week _____ Date _____

GOALS - PLANS - FEELINGS - THOUGHTS - SELF-AFFIRMATIONS
DO-OVER WISHES
ALL GO HERE
FOR YOU!

THANKING MY LUCKY STARS FOR:

_____

_____

_____

LOVE THAT I DID THIS TODAY OR HAVE THIS PLANNED FOR THE DAY:

_____

_____

MAYBE THIS COULD BE IMPROVED:

_____

_____

YES, I ROCK! HERE'S AN AFFIRMATION TO BACK THIS UP:

_____

GOALS ARE GOOD:

_____

_____

JUST HAD TO ADD THIS:

_____

_____

Welcome Back!

Day of the week _____ Date _____

GOALS - PLANS - FEELINGS - THOUGHTS - SELF-AFFIRMATIONS
DO-OVER WISHES
ALL GO HERE
FOR YOU!

THANKING MY LUCKY STARS FOR:

_____

_____

_____

LOVE THAT I DID THIS TODAY OR HAVE THIS PLANNED FOR THE DAY:

_____

_____

MAYBE THIS COULD BE IMPROVED:

_____

_____

YES, I ROCK! HERE'S AN AFFIRMATION TO BACK THIS UP:

_____

GOALS ARE GOOD:

_____

_____

JUST HAD TO ADD THIS:

_____

_____

Welcome Back!

Day of the week _____ Date _____

GOALS - PLANS - FEELINGS - THOUGHTS - SELF-AFFIRMATIONS
DO-OVER WISHES
ALL GO HERE
FOR YOU!

THANKING MY LUCKY STARS FOR:

_____

_____

_____

LOVE THAT I DID THIS TODAY OR HAVE THIS PLANNED FOR THE DAY:

_____

_____

MAYBE THIS COULD BE IMPROVED:

_____

_____

YES, I ROCK! HERE'S AN AFFIRMATION TO BACK THIS UP:

_____

GOALS ARE GOOD:

_____

_____

JUST HAD TO ADD THIS:

_____

_____

Welcome Back!

Day of the week _____ Date _____

GOALS - PLANS - FEELINGS - THOUGHTS - SELF-AFFIRMATIONS
DO-OVER WISHES
ALL GO HERE
FOR YOU!

THANKING MY LUCKY STARS FOR:

_____

_____

_____

LOVE THAT I DID THIS TODAY OR HAVE THIS PLANNED FOR THE DAY:

_____

_____

MAYBE THIS COULD BE IMPROVED:

_____

_____

YES, I ROCK! HERE'S AN AFFIRMATION TO BACK THIS UP:

_____

GOALS ARE GOOD:

_____

_____

JUST HAD TO ADD THIS:

_____

_____

Welcome Back!

Day of the week _____ Date _____

GOALS - PLANS - FEELINGS - THOUGHTS - SELF-AFFIRMATIONS
DO-OVER WISHES
ALL GO HERE
FOR YOU!

THANKING MY LUCKY STARS FOR:

_____

_____

_____

LOVE THAT I DID THIS TODAY OR HAVE THIS PLANNED FOR THE DAY:

_____

_____

MAYBE THIS COULD BE IMPROVED:

_____

_____

YES, I ROCK! HERE'S AN AFFIRMATION TO BACK THIS UP:

_____

GOALS ARE GOOD:

_____

_____

JUST HAD TO ADD THIS:

_____

_____

Welcome Back!

Day of the week _____ Date _____

GOALS - PLANS - FEELINGS - THOUGHTS - SELF-AFFIRMATIONS
DO-OVER WISHES
ALL GO HERE
FOR YOU!

THANKING MY LUCKY STARS FOR:

_____

_____

_____

LOVE THAT I DID THIS TODAY OR HAVE THIS PLANNED FOR THE DAY:

_____

_____

MAYBE THIS COULD BE IMPROVED:

_____

_____

YES, I ROCK! HERE'S AN AFFIRMATION TO BACK THIS UP:

_____

GOALS ARE GOOD:

_____

_____

JUST HAD TO ADD THIS:

_____

_____

Welcome Back!

Day of the week _____ Date _____

GOALS - PLANS - FEELINGS - THOUGHTS - SELF-AFFIRMATIONS
DO-OVER WISHES
ALL GO HERE
FOR YOU!

THANKING MY LUCKY STARS FOR:

_____

_____

_____

LOVE THAT I DID THIS TODAY OR HAVE THIS PLANNED FOR THE DAY:

_____

_____

MAYBE THIS COULD BE IMPROVED:

_____

_____

YES, I ROCK! HERE'S AN AFFIRMATION TO BACK THIS UP:

_____

GOALS ARE GOOD:

_____

_____

JUST HAD TO ADD THIS:

_____

_____

Welcome Back!

Day of the week _____ Date _____

GOALS - PLANS - FEELINGS - THOUGHTS - SELF-AFFIRMATIONS
DO-OVER WISHES
ALL GO HERE
FOR YOU!

THANKING MY LUCKY STARS FOR:

_____

_____

_____

LOVE THAT I DID THIS TODAY OR HAVE THIS PLANNED FOR THE DAY:

_____

_____

MAYBE THIS COULD BE IMPROVED:

_____

_____

YES, I ROCK! HERE'S AN AFFIRMATION TO BACK THIS UP:

_____

GOALS ARE GOOD:

_____

_____

JUST HAD TO ADD THIS:

_____

_____

Welcome Back!

Day of the week _____ Date _____

GOALS - PLANS - FEELINGS - THOUGHTS - SELF-AFFIRMATIONS
DO-OVER WISHES
ALL GO HERE
FOR YOU!

THANKING MY LUCKY STARS FOR:

_____

_____

_____

LOVE THAT I DID THIS TODAY OR HAVE THIS PLANNED FOR THE DAY:

_____

_____

MAYBE THIS COULD BE IMPROVED:

_____

_____

YES, I ROCK! HERE'S AN AFFIRMATION TO BACK THIS UP:

_____

GOALS ARE GOOD:

_____

_____

JUST HAD TO ADD THIS:

_____

_____

Welcome Back!

Day of the week _____ Date _____

GOALS - PLANS - FEELINGS - THOUGHTS - SELF-AFFIRMATIONS
DO-OVER WISHES
ALL GO HERE
FOR YOU!

THANKING MY LUCKY STARS FOR:

_____

_____

_____

LOVE THAT I DID THIS TODAY OR HAVE THIS PLANNED FOR THE DAY:

_____

_____

MAYBE THIS COULD BE IMPROVED:

_____

_____

YES, I ROCK! HERE'S AN AFFIRMATION TO BACK THIS UP:

_____

GOALS ARE GOOD:

_____

_____

JUST HAD TO ADD THIS:

_____

_____

Welcome Back!

Day of the week _____ Date _____

GOALS - PLANS - FEELINGS - THOUGHTS - SELF-AFFIRMATIONS
DO-OVER WISHES
ALL GO HERE
FOR YOU!

THANKING MY LUCKY STARS FOR:

_____

_____

_____

LOVE THAT I DID THIS TODAY OR HAVE THIS PLANNED FOR THE DAY:

_____

_____

MAYBE THIS COULD BE IMPROVED:

_____

_____

YES, I ROCK! HERE'S AN AFFIRMATION TO BACK THIS UP:

_____

GOALS ARE GOOD:

_____

_____

JUST HAD TO ADD THIS:

_____

_____

Welcome Back!

Day of the week _____ Date _____

GOALS - PLANS - FEELINGS - THOUGHTS - SELF-AFFIRMATIONS
DO-OVER WISHES
ALL GO HERE
FOR YOU!

THANKING MY LUCKY STARS FOR:

_____

_____

_____

LOVE THAT I DID THIS TODAY OR HAVE THIS PLANNED FOR THE DAY:

_____

_____

MAYBE THIS COULD BE IMPROVED:

_____

_____

YES, I ROCK! HERE'S AN AFFIRMATION TO BACK THIS UP:

_____

GOALS ARE GOOD:

_____

_____

JUST HAD TO ADD THIS:

_____

_____

Welcome Back!

Day of the week _____ Date _____

GOALS - PLANS - FEELINGS - THOUGHTS - SELF-AFFIRMATIONS
DO-OVER WISHES
ALL GO HERE
FOR YOU!

THANKING MY LUCKY STARS FOR:

_____

_____

_____

LOVE THAT I DID THIS TODAY OR HAVE THIS PLANNED FOR THE DAY:

_____

_____

MAYBE THIS COULD BE IMPROVED:

_____

_____

YES, I ROCK! HERE'S AN AFFIRMATION TO BACK THIS UP:

_____

GOALS ARE GOOD:

_____

_____

JUST HAD TO ADD THIS:

_____

_____

Welcome Back!

Day of the week _____ Date _____

GOALS - PLANS - FEELINGS - THOUGHTS - SELF-AFFIRMATIONS
DO-OVER WISHES
ALL GO HERE
FOR YOU!

THANKING MY LUCKY STARS FOR:

_____

_____

_____

LOVE THAT I DID THIS TODAY OR HAVE THIS PLANNED FOR THE DAY:

_____

_____

MAYBE THIS COULD BE IMPROVED:

_____

_____

YES, I ROCK! HERE'S AN AFFIRMATION TO BACK THIS UP:

_____

GOALS ARE GOOD:

_____

_____

JUST HAD TO ADD THIS:

_____

_____

Welcome Back!

Day of the week _____ Date _____

GOALS - PLANS - FEELINGS - THOUGHTS - SELF-AFFIRMATIONS
DO-OVER WISHES
ALL GO HERE
FOR YOU!

THANKING MY LUCKY STARS FOR:

_____

_____

_____

LOVE THAT I DID THIS TODAY OR HAVE THIS PLANNED FOR THE DAY:

_____

_____

MAYBE THIS COULD BE IMPROVED:

_____

_____

YES, I ROCK! HERE'S AN AFFIRMATION TO BACK THIS UP:

_____

GOALS ARE GOOD:

_____

_____

JUST HAD TO ADD THIS:

_____

_____

Welcome Back!

Day of the week _____ Date _____

GOALS - PLANS - FEELINGS - THOUGHTS - SELF-AFFIRMATIONS
DO-OVER WISHES
ALL GO HERE
FOR YOU!

THANKING MY LUCKY STARS FOR:

_____

_____

_____

LOVE THAT I DID THIS TODAY OR HAVE THIS PLANNED FOR THE DAY:

_____

_____

MAYBE THIS COULD BE IMPROVED:

_____

_____

YES, I ROCK! HERE'S AN AFFIRMATION TO BACK THIS UP:

_____

GOALS ARE GOOD:

_____

_____

JUST HAD TO ADD THIS:

_____

_____

Welcome Back!

Day of the week _____ Date _____

GOALS - PLANS - FEELINGS - THOUGHTS - SELF-AFFIRMATIONS
DO-OVER WISHES
ALL GO HERE
FOR YOU!

THANKING MY LUCKY STARS FOR:

_____

_____

_____

LOVE THAT I DID THIS TODAY OR HAVE THIS PLANNED FOR THE DAY:

_____

_____

MAYBE THIS COULD BE IMPROVED:

_____

_____

YES, I ROCK! HERE'S AN AFFIRMATION TO BACK THIS UP:

_____

GOALS ARE GOOD:

_____

_____

JUST HAD TO ADD THIS:

_____

_____

Welcome Back!

Day of the week _____ Date _____

GOALS - PLANS - FEELINGS - THOUGHTS - SELF-AFFIRMATIONS
DO-OVER WISHES
ALL GO HERE
FOR YOU!

THANKING MY LUCKY STARS FOR:

_____

_____

_____

LOVE THAT I DID THIS TODAY OR HAVE THIS PLANNED FOR THE DAY:

_____

_____

MAYBE THIS COULD BE IMPROVED:

_____

_____

YES, I ROCK! HERE'S AN AFFIRMATION TO BACK THIS UP:

_____

GOALS ARE GOOD:

_____

_____

JUST HAD TO ADD THIS:

_____

_____

Welcome Back!

Day of the week _____ Date _____

GOALS - PLANS - FEELINGS - THOUGHTS - SELF-AFFIRMATIONS
DO-OVER WISHES
ALL GO HERE
FOR YOU!

THANKING MY LUCKY STARS FOR:

_____

_____

_____

LOVE THAT I DID THIS TODAY OR HAVE THIS PLANNED FOR THE DAY:

_____

_____

MAYBE THIS COULD BE IMPROVED:

_____

_____

YES, I ROCK! HERE'S AN AFFIRMATION TO BACK THIS UP:

_____

GOALS ARE GOOD:

_____

_____

JUST HAD TO ADD THIS:

_____

_____

Welcome Back!

Day of the week _____ Date _____

GOALS - PLANS - FEELINGS - THOUGHTS - SELF-AFFIRMATIONS
DO-OVER WISHES
ALL GO HERE
FOR YOU!

THANKING MY LUCKY STARS FOR:

_____

_____

_____

LOVE THAT I DID THIS TODAY OR HAVE THIS PLANNED FOR THE DAY:

_____

_____

MAYBE THIS COULD BE IMPROVED:

_____

_____

YES, I ROCK! HERE'S AN AFFIRMATION TO BACK THIS UP:

_____

GOALS ARE GOOD:

_____

_____

JUST HAD TO ADD THIS:

_____

_____

Welcome Back!

Day of the week _____ Date _____

GOALS - PLANS - FEELINGS - THOUGHTS - SELF-AFFIRMATIONS
DO-OVER WISHES
ALL GO HERE
FOR YOU!

THANKING MY LUCKY STARS FOR:

_____

_____

_____

LOVE THAT I DID THIS TODAY OR HAVE THIS PLANNED FOR THE DAY:

_____

_____

MAYBE THIS COULD BE IMPROVED:

_____

_____

YES, I ROCK! HERE'S AN AFFIRMATION TO BACK THIS UP:

_____

GOALS ARE GOOD:

_____

_____

JUST HAD TO ADD THIS:

_____

_____

Welcome Back!

Day of the week _____ Date _____

GOALS - PLANS - FEELINGS - THOUGHTS - SELF-AFFIRMATIONS
DO-OVER WISHES
ALL GO HERE
FOR YOU!

THANKING MY LUCKY STARS FOR:

_____

_____

_____

LOVE THAT I DID THIS TODAY OR HAVE THIS PLANNED FOR THE DAY:

_____

_____

MAYBE THIS COULD BE IMPROVED:

_____

_____

YES, I ROCK! HERE'S AN AFFIRMATION TO BACK THIS UP:

_____

GOALS ARE GOOD:

_____

_____

JUST HAD TO ADD THIS:

_____

_____

Welcome Back!

Day of the week _____ Date _____

GOALS - PLANS - FEELINGS - THOUGHTS - SELF-AFFIRMATIONS
DO-OVER WISHES
ALL GO HERE
FOR YOU!

THANKING MY LUCKY STARS FOR:

_____

_____

_____

LOVE THAT I DID THIS TODAY OR HAVE THIS PLANNED FOR THE DAY:

_____

_____

MAYBE THIS COULD BE IMPROVED:

_____

_____

YES, I ROCK! HERE'S AN AFFIRMATION TO BACK THIS UP:

_____

GOALS ARE GOOD:

_____

_____

JUST HAD TO ADD THIS:

_____

_____

Welcome Back!

Day of the week _____ Date _____

GOALS - PLANS - FEELINGS - THOUGHTS - SELF-AFFIRMATIONS
DO-OVER WISHES
ALL GO HERE
FOR YOU!

THANKING MY LUCKY STARS FOR:

_____

_____

_____

LOVE THAT I DID THIS TODAY OR HAVE THIS PLANNED FOR THE DAY:

_____

_____

MAYBE THIS COULD BE IMPROVED:

_____

_____

YES, I ROCK! HERE'S AN AFFIRMATION TO BACK THIS UP:

_____

GOALS ARE GOOD:

_____

_____

JUST HAD TO ADD THIS:

_____

_____

Welcome Back!

Day of the week _____ Date _____

GOALS - PLANS - FEELINGS - THOUGHTS - SELF-AFFIRMATIONS
DO-OVER WISHES
ALL GO HERE
FOR YOU!

THANKING MY LUCKY STARS FOR:

_____

_____

_____

LOVE THAT I DID THIS TODAY OR HAVE THIS PLANNED FOR THE DAY:

_____

_____

MAYBE THIS COULD BE IMPROVED:

_____

_____

YES, I ROCK! HERE'S AN AFFIRMATION TO BACK THIS UP:

_____

GOALS ARE GOOD:

_____

_____

JUST HAD TO ADD THIS:

_____

_____

Welcome Back!

Day of the week _____ Date _____

GOALS - PLANS - FEELINGS - THOUGHTS - SELF-AFFIRMATIONS
DO-OVER WISHES
ALL GO HERE
FOR YOU!

THANKING MY LUCKY STARS FOR:

_____

_____

_____

LOVE THAT I DID THIS TODAY OR HAVE THIS PLANNED FOR THE DAY:

_____

_____

MAYBE THIS COULD BE IMPROVED:

_____

_____

YES, I ROCK! HERE'S AN AFFIRMATION TO BACK THIS UP:

_____

GOALS ARE GOOD:

_____

_____

JUST HAD TO ADD THIS:

_____

_____

Welcome Back!

Day of the week _____ Date _____

GOALS - PLANS - FEELINGS - THOUGHTS - SELF-AFFIRMATIONS
DO-OVER WISHES
ALL GO HERE
FOR YOU!

THANKING MY LUCKY STARS FOR:

_____

_____

_____

LOVE THAT I DID THIS TODAY OR HAVE THIS PLANNED FOR THE DAY:

_____

_____

MAYBE THIS COULD BE IMPROVED:

_____

_____

YES, I ROCK! HERE'S AN AFFIRMATION TO BACK THIS UP:

_____

GOALS ARE GOOD:

_____

_____

JUST HAD TO ADD THIS:

_____

_____

Welcome Back!

Day of the week _____ Date _____

GOALS - PLANS - FEELINGS - THOUGHTS - SELF-AFFIRMATIONS
DO-OVER WISHES
ALL GO HERE
FOR YOU!

THANKING MY LUCKY STARS FOR:

_____

_____

_____

LOVE THAT I DID THIS TODAY OR HAVE THIS PLANNED FOR THE DAY:

_____

_____

MAYBE THIS COULD BE IMPROVED:

_____

_____

YES, I ROCK! HERE'S AN AFFIRMATION TO BACK THIS UP:

_____

GOALS ARE GOOD:

_____

_____

JUST HAD TO ADD THIS:

_____

_____

Welcome Back!

Day of the week _____ Date _____

GOALS - PLANS - FEELINGS - THOUGHTS - SELF-AFFIRMATIONS
DO-OVER WISHES
ALL GO HERE
FOR YOU!

THANKING MY LUCKY STARS FOR:

_____

_____

_____

LOVE THAT I DID THIS TODAY OR HAVE THIS PLANNED FOR THE DAY:

_____

_____

MAYBE THIS COULD BE IMPROVED:

_____

_____

YES, I ROCK! HERE'S AN AFFIRMATION TO BACK THIS UP:

_____

GOALS ARE GOOD:

_____

_____

JUST HAD TO ADD THIS:

_____

_____

Welcome Back!

Day of the week _____ Date _____

GOALS - PLANS - FEELINGS - THOUGHTS - SELF-AFFIRMATIONS
DO-OVER WISHES
ALL GO HERE
FOR YOU!

THANKING MY LUCKY STARS FOR:

_____

_____

_____

LOVE THAT I DID THIS TODAY OR HAVE THIS PLANNED FOR THE DAY:

_____

_____

MAYBE THIS COULD BE IMPROVED:

_____

_____

YES, I ROCK! HERE'S AN AFFIRMATION TO BACK THIS UP:

_____

GOALS ARE GOOD:

_____

_____

JUST HAD TO ADD THIS:

_____

_____

Welcome Back!

Day of the week _____ Date _____

GOALS - PLANS - FEELINGS - THOUGHTS - SELF-AFFIRMATIONS
DO-OVER WISHES
ALL GO HERE
FOR YOU!

THANKING MY LUCKY STARS FOR:

_____

_____

_____

LOVE THAT I DID THIS TODAY OR HAVE THIS PLANNED FOR THE DAY:

_____

_____

MAYBE THIS COULD BE IMPROVED:

_____

_____

YES, I ROCK! HERE'S AN AFFIRMATION TO BACK THIS UP:

_____

GOALS ARE GOOD:

_____

_____

JUST HAD TO ADD THIS:

_____

_____

Welcome Back!

Day of the week _____ Date _____

GOALS - PLANS - FEELINGS - THOUGHTS - SELF-AFFIRMATIONS
DO-OVER WISHES
ALL GO HERE
FOR YOU!

THANKING MY LUCKY STARS FOR:

_____

_____

_____

LOVE THAT I DID THIS TODAY OR HAVE THIS PLANNED FOR THE DAY:

_____

_____

MAYBE THIS COULD BE IMPROVED:

_____

_____

YES, I ROCK! HERE'S AN AFFIRMATION TO BACK THIS UP:

_____

GOALS ARE GOOD:

_____

_____

JUST HAD TO ADD THIS:

_____

_____

Welcome Back!

Day of the week _____ Date _____

GOALS - PLANS - FEELINGS - THOUGHTS - SELF-AFFIRMATIONS
DO-OVER WISHES
ALL GO HERE
FOR YOU!

THANKING MY LUCKY STARS FOR:

_____

_____

_____

LOVE THAT I DID THIS TODAY OR HAVE THIS PLANNED FOR THE DAY:

_____

_____

MAYBE THIS COULD BE IMPROVED:

_____

_____

YES, I ROCK! HERE'S AN AFFIRMATION TO BACK THIS UP:

_____

GOALS ARE GOOD:

_____

_____

JUST HAD TO ADD THIS:

_____

_____

Welcome Back!

Day of the week _____ Date _____

GOALS - PLANS - FEELINGS - THOUGHTS - SELF-AFFIRMATIONS
DO-OVER WISHES
ALL GO HERE
FOR YOU!

THANKING MY LUCKY STARS FOR:

_____

_____

_____

LOVE THAT I DID THIS TODAY OR HAVE THIS PLANNED FOR THE DAY:

_____

_____

MAYBE THIS COULD BE IMPROVED:

_____

_____

YES, I ROCK! HERE'S AN AFFIRMATION TO BACK THIS UP:

_____

GOALS ARE GOOD:

_____

_____

JUST HAD TO ADD THIS:

_____

_____

Welcome Back!

Day of the week _____ Date _____

GOALS - PLANS - FEELINGS - THOUGHTS - SELF-AFFIRMATIONS
DO-OVER WISHES
ALL GO HERE
FOR YOU!

THANKING MY LUCKY STARS FOR:

_____

_____

_____

LOVE THAT I DID THIS TODAY OR HAVE THIS PLANNED FOR THE DAY:

_____

_____

MAYBE THIS COULD BE IMPROVED:

_____

_____

YES, I ROCK! HERE'S AN AFFIRMATION TO BACK THIS UP:

_____

GOALS ARE GOOD:

_____

_____

JUST HAD TO ADD THIS:

_____

_____

Welcome Back!

Day of the week _____ Date _____

GOALS - PLANS - FEELINGS - THOUGHTS - SELF-AFFIRMATIONS
DO-OVER WISHES
ALL GO HERE
FOR YOU!

THANKING MY LUCKY STARS FOR:

_____

_____

_____

LOVE THAT I DID THIS TODAY OR HAVE THIS PLANNED FOR THE DAY:

_____

_____

MAYBE THIS COULD BE IMPROVED:

_____

_____

YES, I ROCK! HERE'S AN AFFIRMATION TO BACK THIS UP:

_____

GOALS ARE GOOD:

_____

_____

JUST HAD TO ADD THIS:

_____

_____

Welcome Back!

Day of the week _____ Date _____

GOALS - PLANS - FEELINGS - THOUGHTS - SELF-AFFIRMATIONS
DO-OVER WISHES
ALL GO HERE
FOR YOU!

THANKING MY LUCKY STARS FOR:

_____

_____

_____

LOVE THAT I DID THIS TODAY OR HAVE THIS PLANNED FOR THE DAY:

_____

_____

MAYBE THIS COULD BE IMPROVED:

_____

_____

YES, I ROCK! HERE'S AN AFFIRMATION TO BACK THIS UP:

_____

GOALS ARE GOOD:

_____

_____

JUST HAD TO ADD THIS:

_____

_____

Welcome Back!

Day of the week _____ Date _____

GOALS - PLANS - FEELINGS - THOUGHTS - SELF-AFFIRMATIONS
DO-OVER WISHES
ALL GO HERE
FOR YOU!

THANKING MY LUCKY STARS FOR:

_____

_____

_____

LOVE THAT I DID THIS TODAY OR HAVE THIS PLANNED FOR THE DAY:

_____

_____

MAYBE THIS COULD BE IMPROVED:

_____

_____

YES, I ROCK! HERE'S AN AFFIRMATION TO BACK THIS UP:

_____

GOALS ARE GOOD:

_____

_____

JUST HAD TO ADD THIS:

_____

_____

Welcome Back!

Day of the week _____ Date _____

GOALS - PLANS - FEELINGS - THOUGHTS - SELF-AFFIRMATIONS
DO-OVER WISHES
ALL GO HERE
FOR YOU!

THANKING MY LUCKY STARS FOR:

_____

_____

_____

LOVE THAT I DID THIS TODAY OR HAVE THIS PLANNED FOR THE DAY:

_____

_____

MAYBE THIS COULD BE IMPROVED:

_____

_____

YES, I ROCK! HERE'S AN AFFIRMATION TO BACK THIS UP:

_____

GOALS ARE GOOD:

_____

_____

JUST HAD TO ADD THIS:

_____

_____

Welcome Back!

Day of the week _____ Date _____

GOALS - PLANS - FEELINGS - THOUGHTS - SELF-AFFIRMATIONS
DO-OVER WISHES
ALL GO HERE
FOR YOU!

THANKING MY LUCKY STARS FOR:

_____

_____

_____

LOVE THAT I DID THIS TODAY OR HAVE THIS PLANNED FOR THE DAY:

_____

_____

MAYBE THIS COULD BE IMPROVED:

_____

_____

YES, I ROCK! HERE'S AN AFFIRMATION TO BACK THIS UP:

_____

GOALS ARE GOOD:

_____

_____

JUST HAD TO ADD THIS:

_____

_____

Welcome Back!

Day of the week _____ Date _____

GOALS - PLANS - FEELINGS - THOUGHTS - SELF-AFFIRMATIONS
DO-OVER WISHES
ALL GO HERE
FOR YOU!

THANKING MY LUCKY STARS FOR:

_____

_____

_____

LOVE THAT I DID THIS TODAY OR HAVE THIS PLANNED FOR THE DAY:

_____

_____

MAYBE THIS COULD BE IMPROVED:

_____

_____

YES, I ROCK! HERE'S AN AFFIRMATION TO BACK THIS UP:

_____

GOALS ARE GOOD:

_____

_____

JUST HAD TO ADD THIS:

_____

_____

Welcome Back!

Day of the week _____ Date _____

GOALS - PLANS - FEELINGS - THOUGHTS - SELF-AFFIRMATIONS
DO-OVER WISHES
ALL GO HERE
FOR YOU!

THANKING MY LUCKY STARS FOR:

_____

_____

_____

LOVE THAT I DID THIS TODAY OR HAVE THIS PLANNED FOR THE DAY:

_____

_____

MAYBE THIS COULD BE IMPROVED:

_____

_____

YES, I ROCK! HERE'S AN AFFIRMATION TO BACK THIS UP:

_____

GOALS ARE GOOD:

_____

_____

JUST HAD TO ADD THIS:

_____

_____

Welcome Back!

Day of the week _____ Date _____

GOALS - PLANS - FEELINGS - THOUGHTS - SELF-AFFIRMATIONS
DO-OVER WISHES
ALL GO HERE
FOR YOU!

THANKING MY LUCKY STARS FOR:

_____

_____

_____

LOVE THAT I DID THIS TODAY OR HAVE THIS PLANNED FOR THE DAY:

_____

_____

MAYBE THIS COULD BE IMPROVED:

_____

_____

YES, I ROCK! HERE'S AN AFFIRMATION TO BACK THIS UP:

_____

GOALS ARE GOOD:

_____

_____

JUST HAD TO ADD THIS:

_____

_____

Welcome Back!

Day of the week _____ Date _____

GOALS - PLANS - FEELINGS - THOUGHTS - SELF-AFFIRMATIONS
DO-OVER WISHES
ALL GO HERE
FOR YOU!

THANKING MY LUCKY STARS FOR:

_____

_____

_____

LOVE THAT I DID THIS TODAY OR HAVE THIS PLANNED FOR THE DAY:

_____

_____

MAYBE THIS COULD BE IMPROVED:

_____

_____

YES, I ROCK! HERE'S AN AFFIRMATION TO BACK THIS UP:

_____

GOALS ARE GOOD:

_____

_____

JUST HAD TO ADD THIS:

_____

_____

Welcome Back!

Day of the week _____ Date _____

GOALS - PLANS - FEELINGS - THOUGHTS - SELF-AFFIRMATIONS
DO-OVER WISHES
ALL GO HERE
FOR YOU!

THANKING MY LUCKY STARS FOR:

_____

_____

_____

LOVE THAT I DID THIS TODAY OR HAVE THIS PLANNED FOR THE DAY:

_____

_____

MAYBE THIS COULD BE IMPROVED:

_____

_____

YES, I ROCK! HERE'S AN AFFIRMATION TO BACK THIS UP:

_____

GOALS ARE GOOD:

_____

_____

JUST HAD TO ADD THIS:

_____

_____

Welcome Back!

Day of the week _____ Date _____

GOALS - PLANS - FEELINGS - THOUGHTS - SELF-AFFIRMATIONS
DO-OVER WISHES
ALL GO HERE
FOR YOU!

THANKING MY LUCKY STARS FOR:

_____

_____

_____

LOVE THAT I DID THIS TODAY OR HAVE THIS PLANNED FOR THE DAY:

_____

_____

MAYBE THIS COULD BE IMPROVED:

_____

_____

YES, I ROCK! HERE'S AN AFFIRMATION TO BACK THIS UP:

_____

GOALS ARE GOOD:

_____

_____

JUST HAD TO ADD THIS:

_____

_____

Welcome Back!

Day of the week _____ Date _____

GOALS - PLANS - FEELINGS - THOUGHTS - SELF-AFFIRMATIONS
DO-OVER WISHES
ALL GO HERE
FOR YOU!

THANKING MY LUCKY STARS FOR:

_____
_____
_____

LOVE THAT I DID THIS TODAY OR HAVE THIS PLANNED FOR THE DAY:

_____
_____

MAYBE THIS COULD BE IMPROVED:

_____
_____

YES, I ROCK! HERE'S AN AFFIRMATION TO BACK THIS UP:

_____

GOALS ARE GOOD:

_____
_____

JUST HAD TO ADD THIS:

_____
_____

Welcome Back!

Day of the week _____ Date _____

GOALS - PLANS - FEELINGS - THOUGHTS - SELF-AFFIRMATIONS
DO-OVER WISHES
ALL GO HERE
FOR YOU!

THANKING MY LUCKY STARS FOR:

_____

_____

_____

LOVE THAT I DID THIS TODAY OR HAVE THIS PLANNED FOR THE DAY:

_____

_____

MAYBE THIS COULD BE IMPROVED:

_____

_____

YES, I ROCK! HERE'S AN AFFIRMATION TO BACK THIS UP:

_____

GOALS ARE GOOD:

_____

_____

JUST HAD TO ADD THIS:

_____

_____

Welcome Back!

Day of the week _____ Date _____

GOALS - PLANS - FEELINGS - THOUGHTS - SELF-AFFIRMATIONS
DO-OVER WISHES
ALL GO HERE
FOR YOU!

THANKING MY LUCKY STARS FOR:

_____

_____

_____

LOVE THAT I DID THIS TODAY OR HAVE THIS PLANNED FOR THE DAY:

_____

_____

MAYBE THIS COULD BE IMPROVED:

_____

_____

YES, I ROCK! HERE'S AN AFFIRMATION TO BACK THIS UP:

_____

GOALS ARE GOOD:

_____

_____

JUST HAD TO ADD THIS:

_____

_____

Welcome Back!

Day of the week _____ Date _____

GOALS - PLANS - FEELINGS - THOUGHTS - SELF-AFFIRMATIONS
DO-OVER WISHES
ALL GO HERE
FOR YOU!

THANKING MY LUCKY STARS FOR:

_____

_____

_____

LOVE THAT I DID THIS TODAY OR HAVE THIS PLANNED FOR THE DAY:

_____

_____

MAYBE THIS COULD BE IMPROVED:

_____

_____

YES, I ROCK! HERE'S AN AFFIRMATION TO BACK THIS UP:

_____

GOALS ARE GOOD:

_____

_____

JUST HAD TO ADD THIS:

_____

_____

Welcome Back!

Day of the week _____ Date _____

GOALS - PLANS - FEELINGS - THOUGHTS - SELF-AFFIRMATIONS
DO-OVER WISHES
ALL GO HERE
FOR YOU!

THANKING MY LUCKY STARS FOR:

_____

_____

_____

LOVE THAT I DID THIS TODAY OR HAVE THIS PLANNED FOR THE DAY:

_____

_____

MAYBE THIS COULD BE IMPROVED:

_____

_____

YES, I ROCK! HERE'S AN AFFIRMATION TO BACK THIS UP:

_____

GOALS ARE GOOD:

_____

_____

JUST HAD TO ADD THIS:

_____

_____

Welcome Back!

Day of the week _____ Date _____

GOALS - PLANS - FEELINGS - THOUGHTS - SELF-AFFIRMATIONS
DO-OVER WISHES
ALL GO HERE
FOR YOU!

THANKING MY LUCKY STARS FOR:

_____

_____

_____

LOVE THAT I DID THIS TODAY OR HAVE THIS PLANNED FOR THE DAY:

_____

_____

MAYBE THIS COULD BE IMPROVED:

_____

_____

YES, I ROCK! HERE'S AN AFFIRMATION TO BACK THIS UP:

_____

GOALS ARE GOOD:

_____

_____

JUST HAD TO ADD THIS:

_____

_____

Welcome Back!

Day of the week _____ Date _____

GOALS - PLANS - FEELINGS - THOUGHTS - SELF-AFFIRMATIONS
DO-OVER WISHES
ALL GO HERE
FOR YOU!

THANKING MY LUCKY STARS FOR:

_____

_____

_____

LOVE THAT I DID THIS TODAY OR HAVE THIS PLANNED FOR THE DAY:

_____

_____

MAYBE THIS COULD BE IMPROVED:

_____

_____

YES, I ROCK! HERE'S AN AFFIRMATION TO BACK THIS UP:

_____

GOALS ARE GOOD:

_____

_____

JUST HAD TO ADD THIS:

_____

_____

Welcome Back!

Day of the week _____ Date _____

GOALS - PLANS - FEELINGS - THOUGHTS - SELF-AFFIRMATIONS
DO-OVER WISHES
ALL GO HERE
FOR YOU!

THANKING MY LUCKY STARS FOR:

_____

_____

_____

LOVE THAT I DID THIS TODAY OR HAVE THIS PLANNED FOR THE DAY:

_____

_____

MAYBE THIS COULD BE IMPROVED:

_____

_____

YES, I ROCK! HERE'S AN AFFIRMATION TO BACK THIS UP:

_____

GOALS ARE GOOD:

_____

_____

JUST HAD TO ADD THIS:

_____

_____

Welcome Back!

Day of the week _____ Date _____

GOALS - PLANS - FEELINGS - THOUGHTS - SELF-AFFIRMATIONS
DO-OVER WISHES
ALL GO HERE
FOR YOU!

THANKING MY LUCKY STARS FOR:

_____

_____

_____

LOVE THAT I DID THIS TODAY OR HAVE THIS PLANNED FOR THE DAY:

_____

_____

MAYBE THIS COULD BE IMPROVED:

_____

_____

YES, I ROCK! HERE'S AN AFFIRMATION TO BACK THIS UP:

_____

GOALS ARE GOOD:

_____

_____

JUST HAD TO ADD THIS:

_____

_____

Welcome Back!

Day of the week _____ Date _____

GOALS - PLANS - FEELINGS - THOUGHTS - SELF-AFFIRMATIONS
DO-OVER WISHES
ALL GO HERE
FOR YOU!

THANKING MY LUCKY STARS FOR:

_____

_____

_____

LOVE THAT I DID THIS TODAY OR HAVE THIS PLANNED FOR THE DAY:

_____

_____

MAYBE THIS COULD BE IMPROVED:

_____

_____

YES, I ROCK! HERE'S AN AFFIRMATION TO BACK THIS UP:

_____

GOALS ARE GOOD:

_____

_____

JUST HAD TO ADD THIS:

_____

_____

Welcome Back!

Day of the week _____ Date _____

GOALS - PLANS - FEELINGS - THOUGHTS - SELF-AFFIRMATIONS
DO-OVER WISHES
ALL GO HERE
FOR YOU!

THANKING MY LUCKY STARS FOR:

_____

_____

_____

LOVE THAT I DID THIS TODAY OR HAVE THIS PLANNED FOR THE DAY:

_____

_____

MAYBE THIS COULD BE IMPROVED:

_____

_____

YES, I ROCK! HERE'S AN AFFIRMATION TO BACK THIS UP:

_____

GOALS ARE GOOD:

_____

_____

JUST HAD TO ADD THIS:

_____

_____

Welcome Back!

Day of the week _____ Date _____

GOALS - PLANS - FEELINGS - THOUGHTS - SELF-AFFIRMATIONS
DO-OVER WISHES
ALL GO HERE
FOR YOU!

THANKING MY LUCKY STARS FOR:

_____

_____

_____

LOVE THAT I DID THIS TODAY OR HAVE THIS PLANNED FOR THE DAY:

_____

_____

MAYBE THIS COULD BE IMPROVED:

_____

_____

YES, I ROCK! HERE'S AN AFFIRMATION TO BACK THIS UP:

_____

GOALS ARE GOOD:

_____

_____

JUST HAD TO ADD THIS:

_____

_____

Welcome Back!

Day of the week _____ Date _____

GOALS - PLANS - FEELINGS - THOUGHTS - SELF-AFFIRMATIONS
DO-OVER WISHES
ALL GO HERE
FOR YOU!

THANKING MY LUCKY STARS FOR:

_____

_____

_____

LOVE THAT I DID THIS TODAY OR HAVE THIS PLANNED FOR THE DAY:

_____

_____

MAYBE THIS COULD BE IMPROVED:

_____

_____

YES, I ROCK! HERE'S AN AFFIRMATION TO BACK THIS UP:

_____

GOALS ARE GOOD:

_____

_____

JUST HAD TO ADD THIS:

_____

_____

Welcome Back!

Day of the week _____ Date _____

GOALS - PLANS - FEELINGS - THOUGHTS - SELF-AFFIRMATIONS
DO-OVER WISHES
ALL GO HERE
FOR YOU!

THANKING MY LUCKY STARS FOR:

_____

_____

_____

LOVE THAT I DID THIS TODAY OR HAVE THIS PLANNED FOR THE DAY:

_____

_____

MAYBE THIS COULD BE IMPROVED:

_____

_____

YES, I ROCK! HERE'S AN AFFIRMATION TO BACK THIS UP:

_____

GOALS ARE GOOD:

_____

_____

JUST HAD TO ADD THIS:

_____

_____

Welcome Back!

Day of the week _____ Date _____

GOALS - PLANS - FEELINGS - THOUGHTS - SELF-AFFIRMATIONS
DO-OVER WISHES
ALL GO HERE
FOR YOU!

THANKING MY LUCKY STARS FOR:

_____

_____

_____

LOVE THAT I DID THIS TODAY OR HAVE THIS PLANNED FOR THE DAY:

_____

_____

MAYBE THIS COULD BE IMPROVED:

_____

_____

YES, I ROCK! HERE'S AN AFFIRMATION TO BACK THIS UP:

_____

GOALS ARE GOOD:

_____

_____

JUST HAD TO ADD THIS:

_____

_____

Welcome Back!

Day of the week _____ Date _____

GOALS - PLANS - FEELINGS - THOUGHTS - SELF-AFFIRMATIONS
DO-OVER WISHES
ALL GO HERE
FOR YOU!

THANKING MY LUCKY STARS FOR:

_____

_____

_____

LOVE THAT I DID THIS TODAY OR HAVE THIS PLANNED FOR THE DAY:

_____

_____

MAYBE THIS COULD BE IMPROVED:

_____

_____

YES, I ROCK! HERE'S AN AFFIRMATION TO BACK THIS UP:

_____

GOALS ARE GOOD:

_____

_____

JUST HAD TO ADD THIS:

_____

_____

Welcome Back!

Day of the week _____ Date _____

GOALS - PLANS - FEELINGS - THOUGHTS - SELF-AFFIRMATIONS
DO-OVER WISHES
ALL GO HERE
FOR YOU!

THANKING MY LUCKY STARS FOR:

_____
_____
_____

LOVE THAT I DID THIS TODAY OR HAVE THIS PLANNED FOR THE DAY:

_____
_____

MAYBE THIS COULD BE IMPROVED:

_____
_____

YES, I ROCK! HERE'S AN AFFIRMATION TO BACK THIS UP:

_____

GOALS ARE GOOD:

_____
_____

JUST HAD TO ADD THIS:

_____
_____

Welcome Back!

Day of the week _____ Date _____

GOALS - PLANS - FEELINGS - THOUGHTS - SELF-AFFIRMATIONS
DO-OVER WISHES
ALL GO HERE
FOR YOU!

THANKING MY LUCKY STARS FOR:

_____

_____

_____

LOVE THAT I DID THIS TODAY OR HAVE THIS PLANNED FOR THE DAY:

_____

_____

MAYBE THIS COULD BE IMPROVED:

_____

_____

YES, I ROCK! HERE'S AN AFFIRMATION TO BACK THIS UP:

_____

GOALS ARE GOOD:

_____

_____

JUST HAD TO ADD THIS:

_____

_____

Welcome Back!

Day of the week _____ Date _____

GOALS - PLANS - FEELINGS - THOUGHTS - SELF-AFFIRMATIONS
DO-OVER WISHES
ALL GO HERE
FOR YOU!

THANKING MY LUCKY STARS FOR:

_____

_____

_____

LOVE THAT I DID THIS TODAY OR HAVE THIS PLANNED FOR THE DAY:

_____

_____

MAYBE THIS COULD BE IMPROVED:

_____

_____

YES, I ROCK! HERE'S AN AFFIRMATION TO BACK THIS UP:

_____

GOALS ARE GOOD:

_____

_____

JUST HAD TO ADD THIS:

_____

_____

Welcome Back!

Day of the week _____ Date _____

GOALS - PLANS - FEELINGS - THOUGHTS - SELF-AFFIRMATIONS
DO-OVER WISHES
ALL GO HERE
FOR YOU!

THANKING MY LUCKY STARS FOR:

_____

_____

_____

LOVE THAT I DID THIS TODAY OR HAVE THIS PLANNED FOR THE DAY:

_____

_____

MAYBE THIS COULD BE IMPROVED:

_____

_____

YES, I ROCK! HERE'S AN AFFIRMATION TO BACK THIS UP:

_____

GOALS ARE GOOD:

_____

_____

JUST HAD TO ADD THIS:

_____

_____

Welcome Back!

Day of the week _____ Date _____

GOALS - PLANS - FEELINGS - THOUGHTS - SELF-AFFIRMATIONS
DO-OVER WISHES
ALL GO HERE
FOR YOU!

THANKING MY LUCKY STARS FOR:

_____

_____

_____

LOVE THAT I DID THIS TODAY OR HAVE THIS PLANNED FOR THE DAY:

_____

_____

MAYBE THIS COULD BE IMPROVED:

_____

_____

YES, I ROCK! HERE'S AN AFFIRMATION TO BACK THIS UP:

_____

GOALS ARE GOOD:

_____

_____

JUST HAD TO ADD THIS:

_____

_____

Welcome Back!

Day of the week _____ Date _____

GOALS - PLANS - FEELINGS - THOUGHTS - SELF-AFFIRMATIONS
DO-OVER WISHES
ALL GO HERE
FOR YOU!

THANKING MY LUCKY STARS FOR:

_____

_____

_____

LOVE THAT I DID THIS TODAY OR HAVE THIS PLANNED FOR THE DAY:

_____

_____

MAYBE THIS COULD BE IMPROVED:

_____

_____

YES, I ROCK! HERE'S AN AFFIRMATION TO BACK THIS UP:

_____

GOALS ARE GOOD:

_____

_____

JUST HAD TO ADD THIS:

_____

_____

Welcome Back!

Day of the week _____ Date _____

GOALS - PLANS - FEELINGS - THOUGHTS - SELF-AFFIRMATIONS
DO-OVER WISHES
ALL GO HERE
FOR YOU!

THANKING MY LUCKY STARS FOR:

_____

_____

_____

LOVE THAT I DID THIS TODAY OR HAVE THIS PLANNED FOR THE DAY:

_____

_____

MAYBE THIS COULD BE IMPROVED:

_____

_____

YES, I ROCK! HERE'S AN AFFIRMATION TO BACK THIS UP:

_____

GOALS ARE GOOD:

_____

_____

JUST HAD TO ADD THIS:

_____

_____

Welcome Back!

Day of the week _____ Date _____

GOALS - PLANS - FEELINGS - THOUGHTS - SELF-AFFIRMATIONS
DO-OVER WISHES
ALL GO HERE
FOR YOU!

THANKING MY LUCKY STARS FOR:

_____

_____

_____

LOVE THAT I DID THIS TODAY OR HAVE THIS PLANNED FOR THE DAY:

_____

_____

MAYBE THIS COULD BE IMPROVED:

_____

_____

YES, I ROCK! HERE'S AN AFFIRMATION TO BACK THIS UP:

_____

GOALS ARE GOOD:

_____

_____

JUST HAD TO ADD THIS:

_____

_____

Welcome Back!

Day of the week _____ Date _____

GOALS - PLANS - FEELINGS - THOUGHTS - SELF-AFFIRMATIONS
DO-OVER WISHES
ALL GO HERE
FOR YOU!

THANKING MY LUCKY STARS FOR:

_____

_____

_____

LOVE THAT I DID THIS TODAY OR HAVE THIS PLANNED FOR THE DAY:

_____

_____

MAYBE THIS COULD BE IMPROVED:

_____

_____

YES, I ROCK! HERE'S AN AFFIRMATION TO BACK THIS UP:

_____

GOALS ARE GOOD:

_____

_____

JUST HAD TO ADD THIS:

_____

_____

Welcome Back!

Day of the week _____ Date _____

GOALS - PLANS - FEELINGS - THOUGHTS - SELF-AFFIRMATIONS
DO-OVER WISHES
ALL GO HERE
FOR YOU!

THANKING MY LUCKY STARS FOR:

_____

_____

_____

LOVE THAT I DID THIS TODAY OR HAVE THIS PLANNED FOR THE DAY:

_____

_____

MAYBE THIS COULD BE IMPROVED:

_____

_____

YES, I ROCK! HERE'S AN AFFIRMATION TO BACK THIS UP:

_____

GOALS ARE GOOD:

_____

_____

JUST HAD TO ADD THIS:

_____

_____

Welcome Back!

Day of the week _____ Date _____

GOALS - PLANS - FEELINGS - THOUGHTS - SELF-AFFIRMATIONS
DO-OVER WISHES
ALL GO HERE
FOR YOU!

THANKING MY LUCKY STARS FOR:

_____

_____

_____

LOVE THAT I DID THIS TODAY OR HAVE THIS PLANNED FOR THE DAY:

_____

_____

MAYBE THIS COULD BE IMPROVED:

_____

_____

YES, I ROCK! HERE'S AN AFFIRMATION TO BACK THIS UP:

_____

GOALS ARE GOOD:

_____

_____

JUST HAD TO ADD THIS:

_____

_____

Welcome Back!

Day of the week _____ Date _____

GOALS - PLANS - FEELINGS - THOUGHTS - SELF-AFFIRMATIONS
DO-OVER WISHES
ALL GO HERE
FOR YOU!

THANKING MY LUCKY STARS FOR:

_____

_____

_____

LOVE THAT I DID THIS TODAY OR HAVE THIS PLANNED FOR THE DAY:

_____

_____

MAYBE THIS COULD BE IMPROVED:

_____

_____

YES, I ROCK! HERE'S AN AFFIRMATION TO BACK THIS UP:

_____

GOALS ARE GOOD:

_____

_____

JUST HAD TO ADD THIS:

_____

_____

Welcome Back!

Day of the week _____ Date _____

GOALS - PLANS - FEELINGS - THOUGHTS - SELF-AFFIRMATIONS
DO-OVER WISHES
ALL GO HERE
FOR YOU!

THANKING MY LUCKY STARS FOR:

_____

_____

_____

LOVE THAT I DID THIS TODAY OR HAVE THIS PLANNED FOR THE DAY:

_____

_____

MAYBE THIS COULD BE IMPROVED:

_____

_____

YES, I ROCK! HERE'S AN AFFIRMATION TO BACK THIS UP:

_____

GOALS ARE GOOD:

_____

_____

JUST HAD TO ADD THIS:

_____

_____

Welcome Back!

Day of the week _____ Date _____

GOALS - PLANS - FEELINGS - THOUGHTS - SELF-AFFIRMATIONS
DO-OVER WISHES
ALL GO HERE
FOR YOU!

THANKING MY LUCKY STARS FOR:

_____

_____

_____

LOVE THAT I DID THIS TODAY OR HAVE THIS PLANNED FOR THE DAY:

_____

_____

MAYBE THIS COULD BE IMPROVED:

_____

_____

YES, I ROCK! HERE'S AN AFFIRMATION TO BACK THIS UP:

_____

GOALS ARE GOOD:

_____

_____

JUST HAD TO ADD THIS:

_____

_____

One Season at a Time

Available in a growing number of editions.
Each edition contains the same journal format, but individually selected images.

Available late fall 2022:

~ Blue hyacinth edition

Coming early winter 2022:

~ Mauve roses edition

Personalize your journaling experience.

Select the same or different edition for your next season of self-discovery.

~

Don't miss out!

Sign up for E. B. Lee's newsletter to find out when new editions of *One Season at a Time* become available: www.eblee.me

~

A simple request, please...

If you have enjoyed *One Season at A Time*, please let others know.

By leaving a rating or review on the journal's sales page online, you help others decide if this is a good purchase choice for them.

It's easy to do.

Either leave a rating with stars only, or add a line on one thing you like about *One Season at A Time*.